Finding
and
Keeping
Romantic Love

Relationship Tips for People over Fifty

PAULINE G. EVERETTE, LMSW, PHD

BALBOA.
PRESS

A DIVISION OF HAY HOUSE

Balboa Press books may be ordered through booksellers or by contacting:

Balboa Press
A Division of Hay House
1663 Liberty Drive
Bloomington, IN 47403
www.balboapress.com
1 (877) 407-4847

Because of the dynamic nature of the Internet, any web addresses or links contained in this book may have changed since publication and may no longer be valid. The views expressed in this work are solely those of the author and do not necessarily reflect the views of the publisher, and the publisher hereby disclaims any responsibility for them.

The author of this book does not dispense medical advice or prescribe the use of any technique as a form of treatment for physical, emotional, or medical problems without the advice of a physician, either directly or indirectly. The intent of the author is only to offer information of a general nature to help you in your quest for emotional and spiritual well-being. In the event you use any of the information in this book for yourself, which is your constitutional right, the author and the publisher assume no responsibility for your actions.

Any people depicted in stock imagery provided by Thinkstock are models, and such images are being used for illustrative purposes only. Certain stock imagery © Thinkstock.

Print information available on the last page.

ISBN: 978-1-5043-4307-7 (sc)
ISBN: 978-1-5043-4308-4 (e)

Library of Congress Control Number: 2015916830

Balboa Press rev. date: 07/21/2016

Contents

Dedication

This book is dedicated to lovers and would be lovers. It is my desire to ignite a flame of hope in the possibility of creating a strong emotional connection between romantic partner.

Acknowledgments

I would like to acknowledge the many clients who have over the years entrusted me with their deepest hopes, dreams, and fears.

I would like to acknowledge Jan Hill my coach for her guidance and support from the beginning to the end. This project would not have happened without her.

I would like to acknowledge Dee Jaye Clark, Eva Ross, Sharon Moorehead, Roxanne Barzone and KC Vansen, friends who encouraged me along the way.

I would like to acknowledge all my teachers, too numerous to list.

Last, but never least, I would like to thank my life partner of over 40 years, Ken Eichhorn, who is always there to pick up the slack allowing me to push my boundaries.

Introduction

For over 30 years I have had the privilege of sitting with countless fellow seekers (some call them clients) bearing witness to their suffering, their victories, and their redemptions. My experience as a psychotherapist has taught me that seekers come with similar problems disguised in various forms.

As the seekers and I join forces and patiently and gently undo, deconstruct, and closely examine life stories, it always comes down to people wanting to be happy. The people who come to me are often feeling disconnected, unhappy, unloved, ignored, and disregarded. Together we sort through the chapters that compose their unique stories to arrive at a good idea of what paths may lead to a clearing—a place of new possibilities.

When seekers come as couples, they often want better communication, more affection, a greater sense of connection to their partner, and less bickering. Many grieve the absence of romance in their relationships. For others, the idea of romance is a vague recollection triggered occasionally by a scent, a song, or a memory. Without fail, couples are convinced that life would be better if only their partner would change. Sometimes couples come hoping to heal a relationship seriously wounded by infidelity. In those cases, conventional wisdom tells them that the offending partner is clearly to blame for the sadness and unhappiness they are experiencing while they are clearly the victim. These couples find themselves in the midst of a storm that threatens to tear their lives apart.

Sometimes singles, usually women, come speaking of feeling sad, lonely, isolated, and wounded by the men who left their lives. They feel conflicted—fearful of trying again, while simultaneously longing to be connected to a loving romantic life partner.

Contrary to folk wisdom, no matter their age, people have the ability to change—to create a life more to their liking. Many of my most valuable life lessons have been learned and more fully integrated into my life after reaching age fifty! Many of the people I see in my practice are over fifty. A sizable number of them are either in a relationship that is waning and losing its vigor, or are singles (divorced or never married) who are considering dating but have lots of fears and bad associations from past relationships that disappointed.

This book grows out of my deep desire to share key life lessons that have grown out of my studies, spiritual practices, lived experiences, and sitting with fellow seekers in reflection and compassion. These experiences have convinced me that we can all learn to be more connected, more compassionate with ourselves and others, and more willing to take the chances that romantic relationships require.

Over the years, I have studied psychoanalytic theory, Neuro Linguistic Programming, Buddhist Psychology, Imago Therapy, yoga, mindfulness, transformational learning theory, peace and conflict theory and practice, and the list goes on. I have done silent retreats in the jungles of South India, studied indigenous spirituality in West Africa, and I practice yoga and mindfulness meditation daily. I still teach an occasional yoga class. But, in fact, my 40 years of marriage has been my most direct teacher. My marriage/romantic partnering has taught me more about being in relationship than any other single endeavor.

My comments, observations, and suggestions are informed by my experience as a psychotherapist, life coach, mentor, romantic partner, and fellow seeker.

Each chapter of this book is devoted to a topic that is referred to as a tip but is in many ways a skill. Each chapter contains a letter from a fictional client addressing the specific topic. The fictionalized letters are included to make the topic come alive and show practical application. The letter writers are fictional to protect and honor the confidentiality of my former and current clients. My responses to the letter writers attempt to illuminate the topic by asking the writers to be vulnerable, responsible, brave, and compassionate. This is done from a point of view that assumes we are each capable of having and giving the romantic love we seek.

To make the most of the reading experience, I invite you to reflect on the exercises found at the end of each chapter. Each set of exercises is designed to help you personalize the reading and apply the tips to your life.

CHAPTER 1

The Gremlin: Facing the Chatter

Tip: Get Acquainted with Your Gremlin

Each of us has an internal critic. We'll call that internal critic the gremlin. Much has been written about the gremlin. Basically, the gremlin refers to recurring negative self- talk. The gremlin can show up at the most inopportune times. It shows up as a mood buster, a fear monger, a naysayer, or a nag. The gremlin reminds us of past failures, warns us to play small, and threatens to remind us of all our faults and perceived short- comings.

For those over fifty and not in a relationship, the gremlin may be whispering, "No way, no how, too late, what is the chance of meeting someone now?", "Online dating may have worked for some people but it would never work for me," or "It is just too much work." For those in lackluster romantic relationships, the gremlin may murmur "Why not just leave well enough alone? It's only natural to lose the intensity and excitement you felt earlier in the relationship."

The gremlin can be very convincing. After years of struggling with my own gremlins and helping others navigate their way through the maze of Gremlinville, I have become convinced that the best way to manage the gremlin is to become aware of his presence, become familiar with the various ways he shows up, and befriend him. YES!!!!!!!!!! Befriend him. Give him a name. I have decided to refer to my gremlin as 'Ms. Chatty'. I have come to think of her as a friend seeking to protect me. Consider it a friend on steroids who needs to be managed. I recall a mentor who suggested we thank the gremlin for sharing and then gently dismiss her. Gremlins chatter about many areas of one's life, including relationships. Even though protective in intent, if left unchecked, a gremlin can interfere with one's efforts to be a partner in an exciting, mutually loving, romantic relationship.

This letter from Anne illustrates this point. Anne is in a relatively new marriage. She has noticed that things are not as good between her and her husband as they used to be. Notice the role the gremlin plays in Anne's thoughts and feelings, and how her beliefs and attitude (informed by the gremlin) are damaging her relationship with her spouse.

Dear Dr. Amor,

I am 55 and my husband is 62. We have been married for three years. It is our second marriage. We were both previously married and divorced. We made a lot of mistakes in our previous marriages that we do not want to repeat. We are financially comfortable and looking forward to retirement in a few years. Life should be good. But, it is not.

I have never been comfortable with my husband's friends. Many of them are physicians and other professionals. I have always struggled with feelings of inadequacy especially when it comes to my intellect and lack of credentials. I work in the hospital, where I met my husband, as an administrative assistant to the chief of surgery. Because of this I feel awkward at social gatherings with his friends and either talk too much or just clam up. My husband really enjoys parties and socializing with his friends and colleagues. Because of my discomfort, we are socializing less and less. I feel this is driving us apart. We are starting to bicker and we are not nearly as affectionate with each other as we once were. I love my husband and I want our marriage to last. I know he loves me, but I must admit I am a little disappointed that my husband places so much importance on his friendships and is not as sympathetic toward me as I think he should be. What should I do, just suck it up and go and pretend to enjoy myself?

Anne

Dear Anne,

There are a number of things to consider. Before that, I want to commend you for being proactive about your relationship issues. Second marriages provide a chance for a "do over", informed by the mistakes and successes from previous relationships. I suspect the gremlin has taken up residence in your thoughts. I have a couple of suggestions. First, go to Martin Seligman's web page (https://www.

authentichappiness.sas.upenn.edu/) and take the VIA Character Strengths Survey. The survey will identify your top five strengths—known as signature strengths. I encourage you to get familiar with your strengths. Write your strengths down and post them in a place where you are forced to see them regularly. I keep my list on a corkboard right over my work desk. On those days when the gremlin is busy chatting away, I find it helpful to remind myself of my five signature strengths.

The gremlin tends to think in terms of good and bad, black and white. From your letter, I assume your gremlin has you attacking yourself for lacking the credentials that your husband and his peers have.

Listen carefully to your internal chatter--what exactly is the gremlin whispering about your worth as compared to the worth of your husband and his peers? Write it down. Now, ask yourself, "Is it true?" Is it absolutely true that you are any less a valuable human being because you are not a physician? How would your life be different if you did not have those thoughts?

It sounds as if your husband is socially gregarious--you, not so much. If this is true across the board and not just in situations that involve his professional friends, you may be more of an introvert while he may be more of an extrovert. Extroverts and introverts have very different ways of being comfortable in social situations. As an introvert, you may prefer to listen and observe, and talk to people one on one, avoiding small talk. What would it be like if you told yourself that is okay—that introverts bring strengths and value to the party just as extroverts do? What would it be like if you went to a social gathering with your husband intent on just being you, open to the possibility of having a good time without altering your personality or pretending to be someone you are not?

People are different-- some people like apple pie and others prefer cherry pie. Most of the time we accept such differences as harmless. You write that your reluctance to join your husband in socializing with his peers may be straining your relationship. Have you discussed this with your husband? Or, is this an assumption? Is the fact that you and your husband and many of his friends have different professional backgrounds the real issue, or is it how the difference makes you feel? Talking with your husband about your insecurities, and we all have them, can open a new level of intimacy between the two of you.

Answering the following questions may help you get started:

Where will you post your strengths?_____

When will you have a talk with your husband?_____

What do you want to gain from having the talk?_____

Reader Activities

Readers go to VIA strengths survey and take the survey. The survey will reveal your top strengths. The strengths are traits you possess.

List your top five signature strengths:

1.
2.
3.
4.
5.

Keep them handy.

For more information about the gremlin go to__http:// inspiredcommitment.com/dumping-relationship-baggage/ taming-your-gremlins

For more information about introverts visit_https://www. psychologytoday.com/basics/introversion

Reader Reflections

What is your gremlin saying that sabotages your romantic relationship(s)?

Which of your strengths will be most useful in helping you respond appropriately to the misinformation passed on by the gremlin?

CHAPTER 2

Communication: On the Road to Better Understanding

Tip: Say what needs to be said with integrity, bravery, compassion, and truth. Listen with openness while seeking to understand.

Open, honest, brave, and compassionate communication is good medicine for romantic relationships. When couples come to see me the first question I ask, is "What brings you in?" Inevitably they mention communication. "We just don't communicate" is the much repeated report. Often neither person has felt, heard, or understood for a long time. After a while, these couples stop trying to communicate. It becomes easier to avoid trying. To protect what is left of their self-esteem, they avoid talking about anything but the most ordinary and routine matters.

The elephant in the living room (the problem) is not disturbed, for fear it will tear the place apart. One of my first tasks is to help the couple understand that there are powerful reasons why they have stopped communicating and that the lack of communication is a sign that something has gone wrong. Their willingness to delve into the stuff that caused them to stop talking, listening, and responding is a measure of how successful they'll be at resuscitating their romance.

Merriam Webster's Collegiate Dictionary, 10th edition, defines communication as "To transmit information, thought, or feeling so that it is satisfactorily received or understood." And, while we typically think of communication as involving speaking, social scientists know that much of communication is nonverbal. Dr. Albert Mehrabian, author of <u>Silent Messages</u>, conducted several studies on nonverbal communication. He found that 7% of any message is conveyed through words, 38% through certain vocal elements, and 55% through nonverbal elements (facial expressions, gestures, posture, etc). Subtracting the 7% for actual verbal content means that 93% of meaning is communicated non-verbally. If we are not considering our nonverbal communication habits, we are overlooking the most essential part of how we communicate. To learn more about Dr. Mehrabian work visit http://www.kaaj.com/psych/.

I am going to assume that we would all like to be better communicators. After all, effective communication skills contribute to healthy romantic relationships. To increase the chances of being effective communicators there are some habits that need to be broken because they are barriers to effective communication.

Barriers to effectively communicating with a partner are:

- Fear of rejection
- Avoidance of vulnerability
- Rushing to judgment
- Speaking harshly

Effective communicators will avoid:

- Giving unwanted advice
- Moving prematurely to problem solving
- Changing the subject (*Linda Wilcox, Harvard University*)

I would add that effective communicators:

- Benefit from knowing their preferred communication style
- Speak what needs to be said in an open and compassionate manner
- Listen with the intention of understanding what the other has to say

Communication can go wrong for many reasons . But, often when communication derails, it is because one or both partners are hiding. When people feel vulnerable they become self-protective and shields go up. This is illustrated in the following letter from Ylan.

Dear Dr. Amor,

Jon and I have been dating for six months. For the most part things are going really well. But, there is one small thing that bothers me. Jon has a habit of being late. Sometimes as little as 15 minutes, at other times as much as an hour. Sometimes he calls or texts, other times not. This makes me angry. When I try to discuss it with him he brushes it off and promises to do better. He sulks for a while after I bring it up. I feel like I am turning into a nag. I am stumped. Why can't we just have a conversation about it? Maybe if I understood his reasoning I could be more understanding and patient. But, he won't open up and talk about it. What should I do?

~

Dear Ylan,

I get the impression that you see promise in this relationship and that you are interested in pursuing it. We can only speculate about Jon's unwillingness to discuss his chronic tardiness. Here are some things to consider. Communication scholars have identified certain communication styles. Many agree that there are three basic styles of communication. They are:

- Aggressive
- Passive
- Assertive

Aggressive communicators tend to be in your face, verbally and non-verbally. For example, an aggressive communicator may shake his finger, distort his face, raise his voice and stare. He or she may come across as a bully. The passive communicator is more likely to make himself small, cower, have a slumped posture, and a blank expression. He or she may come across as disinterested. Finally, there is the assertive communication style. This style is characterized by having an open demeanor, making eye contact, listening, and being engaged. I think you can see the value in having an assertive approach to communication in your romantic relationship. We develop our 'go to' communication style for any number of reasons ranging from our individual personality traits to societal expectations. Whatever the reason, it is clear that how we communicate will affect the quality and longevity of our romantic relationships. We don't know why Jon has developed a style that appears to be passive. The question is-- how do you best respond in the situation you describe?

To learn more about your communication style visit **http://www.communication-styles.com/communication-style-survey-instructions.html**

Once you have learned your preferred communication style, ask yourself, "Is this style likely to contribute to an open, honest, and compassionate arena for communication?" If your answer to that question is yes, you will also want to consider how and when you introduce the discussion of

Jon's tardiness and its effect on you. Communication 101 instructs:

- Use "I" statements. When you begin a conversation with "You" the other person is much more likely to feel defensive and react by disengaging.
- Choose a time to discuss your concerns that is likely to be free of distractions.
- Bring the topic up when you are not feeling overly stressed about it.
- Consider humor. Humor can help diffuse a potentially uncomfortable situation. Use caution here. Humor can sometimes be misunderstood.
- Remember to stay in your lane. There is nothing you can do to change Jon. You can only show up to the discussion with the intention of being open and honest and delivering your message with compassion.
- Before having the conversation ask yourself, "What do I want to convey? What is my desired outcome? Is his continued tardiness a deal breaker? Is his unwillingness to discuss uncomfortable topics a deal breaker?"

Reader Activities:

Go to http://www.communication-styles.com/communication-style-survey-instructions.html and take your communication style survey.

What did you learn? _____

How will you apply it to become an even more effective communicator?

_____

_____

_____

Consider having your partner take the survey and compare your results.

Based on your results, make a commitment to three communication goals.

_____

_____

_____

Finally, revisit your VIA strengths identified in Chapter One. Write your answer to the question

"How might my strengths help me become a more effective communicator?"

CHAPTER 3

Conflict Management: Yes We Can

Tip: Avoid denial. Facing conflict head on, with the intention of compassionate communication, goes a long way toward resolving conflict and bringing you closer. Intend the good for all involved.

Would you like to manage conflict in a more effective manner? Have you ever thought or been told you have a problem with anger? Do you find yourself dreading situations where you have to talk with someone about a sensitive topic when you know there are differences of opinion? Or, maybe you are the one others go out of the way to avoid because they fear you will overreact. If any of this describes you, please keep reading. There are things you can do to become a more effective conflict manager.

Conflict Defined

Long lasting romantic relationships are bound to experience conflict. Having the skills and tools necessary to manage conflict can make the difference between conflict managing you or you managing conflict. Conflict can be defined in several different ways. The following definition will help us start our discussion on the same page. According to YARN (1999), "conflict refers narrowly to a disagreement. . ." the act of disagreeing. Conflict may or may not involve hostile action. Scholars agree that we tend to have a preferred conflict management style. Your conflict style is your "go to" way of dealing with conflict.

Conflict Styles

Wilmot and Hocker (2013) suggest our preferred conflict style is likely a combination of genetics, life experiences, and family influences. Most experts in the field of conflict describe five conflict styles:

- Accommodating
- Avoiding
- Competing
- Compromising
- Collaborating

Briefly, people who *accommodate* can give in too quickly. They tend to be passive in the face of conflict. *Avoiders* are similar. They go out of their way to avoid conflict. People who approach conflict from a *competitive* angle value holding their own and standing their ground. They may actually enjoy conflict, as it gives them an opportunity to flex their muscles. *Compromisers* prefer getting past the conflict quickly and efficiently. They are eager to split the difference. Those who prefer a *collaborating* approach are willing to be patient and explore all aspects of the conflict seeking a win/win solution.

Experts in conflict often speak of the benefits of a collaborative style of conflict management. Indeed, much of the time a collaborative approach to conflict is desirable. There are, however, times when other styles are best. For example, in a heated situation where tempers are flared, avoidance may be the best response to the situation. In contrast, in an emergent situation (no time to lose) an assertive approach may be the best response.

Once you become aware of your preferred conflict style, you have the advantage of being able to modify it to fit the occasion. I think about it like this: many of our behaviors are like habits. A habit is like a default. Each time I turn on my computer and go to 'Word', the font is set at size 12 Times Roman. Most of the time that works for me. Sometimes, however, a different font and size is preferred. When that is the case, I have to go to the tool bar and manually change the font and size. The same holds true with many of our habitual ways of responding to conflict situations. We want to have some choice in how we respond rather than mindlessly doing what comes naturally.

Views of Conflict

Many of us have come to think of conflict in negative terms, such as, bad, to be avoided, dangerous, scary and so on. In fact the body seems to support this view. It seems hard-wired to respond to conflict as a threat. Being in the throes of negative conflict, screaming, swearing, threatening, can bring up a flood of emotions that prompt the fight or flight response. The fight or flight syndrome refers to the body's physiological response to a physical or emotional threat. As the term implies, the body gears up to fight its way out of the situation or, if that is not feasible, run away. It seems to be human nature to attack when feeling attacked. Imagine for a moment what this can do to our romantic relationships. Fortunately, we as human beings have the ability to override this biological tendency and shift our perspective on conflict.

Conflict as an Opportunity

Conflict is a naturally occurring reaction to different needs, wants, and beliefs. Any two people, lovers included, are bound to have different viewpoints from time to time. So, rather than trying to avoid conflict, a better use of your energy is to learn to manage it. Part of managing it is to change how you view it. Think of conflict as an opportunity.

Many years ago, I decided to formally study conflict management and mediation, a process designed to resolve conflict. Little did I know at the time that studying conflict would shift my perspective on conflict. Over time, I learned to view conflict as an opportunity. When handled properly, conflict can actually take your relationship to a new level. You and your partner learn that the relationship is sound enough to withstand conflict. This can be particularly reassuring to couples in the early stage of their relationship.

Costs of Avoiding Conflict

When we value our relationships and want them to thrive and be safe, we can erroneously believe that the best way to keep them safe is by avoiding conflict, ignoring conflict, and downplaying differences that need to be recognized. This way of thinking about conflict and reacting to it actually puts the relationship at greater risk for failure. Why? Because problems that need attention can go unaddressed, fester and eventually drive a wedge between people.

Benefits of Addressing Conflict

Avoiding conflict reminds me of a couple I used to see in couple counseling. Harry was annoyed that Jenny "interrupted" him when he was speaking. Yet, over the seven years of their relationship, he had never brought it to her attention. As we explored their concerns, it became obvious to them (and me) that Harry had many small grievances that he never mentioned to Jenny.

It bothered him that she interrupted him, and that she never initiated sex, among other things. He never mentioned it, for fear Jenny would not understand and withdraw her love and affection. This was a pattern Harry had witnessed in his family growing up. So, instead of bringing his concerns to her attention, Harry sucked it up and developed what I call a slush fund of grievances. His slush fund contained all his unvoiced concerns about how he perceived Jenny treated him. Eventually, his slush fund became full. His unexpressed grievances showed up in passive aggressive behavior that left Jenny perplexed and confused.

Part of my work with the couple involved helping Harry become aware of his passive approach to conflict, and how that approach harmed the relationship. Harry learned that he could express concerns to Jenny and still love her and be loved by her. This made a positive difference in their relationship. They learned that it is perfectly natural to have conflict, and that conflict can be managed and not cause harm to the relationship. As a result, they grew even closer and experienced a deeper sense of intimacy than ever before.

Many people fear conflict because they do not have a clear idea of how to manage it effectively. The 'I win-you lose' (zero sum) approach to conflict is alive and well. When helped to think beyond the 'I win-you lose' paradigm, couples discover new ways of approaching conflict that opens new realms of possibility. This is illustrated by a letter from Mary:

Dear Dr. Amor,

My partner Arthur and I are in a committed long term relationship. We have lived together for 13 years. I recently settled into the job of my dreams. I plan to retire within the next five years and this job will position me to develop a lucrative consulting position after I retire. I should be celebrating, right? Wrong. Timing could not be worse. Arthur was just offered a promotion that will require him to live abroad for the next two years, at minimum. We are stumped. We want to be together and we also want to take advantage of the career opportunities available to us. Neither of us is comfortable giving up what seems to be the chance of a lifetime. But, I love this man. I have thought about passing on the job, but I do not want to risk harboring resentments about doing so, down the road. We would love to hear your thoughts about how we might approach this dilemma.

Mary

Dear Mary,

Kudos to you for realizing this situation will require a thoughtful joint effort between you and your partner. I fear there is no easy answer, but here are some things to consider and a process that may help illuminate the situation. Many years ago, I developed a mnemonic device to help my students remember the steps involved in a common problem solving process.

Who knows, perhaps I was hungry on that day--the mnemonic is PASTA.

The **P**=Problem--state the problem

The **A**=Analyze and discuss the differences

The **S**=Identify various solutions

The **T**= Trade-offs/negotiate

The **A**=Agreement come to a mutually agreeable agreement.

To get you started, a rough statement of the problem is:

Problem-- You and Arthur want to be together but existing career opportunities that you each want are located in different countries.

Analyze the Differences-- It appears that if you don't take advantage of the career opportunity, you will sacrifice your long- range career plans and fear you will feel resentment toward your partner in the long-run.

Solutions--Brain storming solutions is a good way of thinking outside the box and coming up with new and innovative solutions. This is something you and Arthur could do together. For example:

1. Arthur could turn down the promotion and stay put.
2. You could quit your job and accompany Arthur overseas.
3. You could stay in your job and Arthur could take the promotion.

4. You could look into other opportunities that would position you well for your post retirement plans.
5. You could stay put, Arthur could take the promotion, and together you could come up with a plan to see each other as often as possible and stay connected.
6. You could rethink your post retirement plans.
7. You could quit your job, and Arthur could quit his job and together you could re-envision your career goals and options.

Do not limit yourselves when creating the list. If it comes to mind, write it down. The next step will allow you to narrow your list down to workable options.

Trade offs/negotiate--After creating your list, read through and highlight the top three options you would like to explore more closely. Consider the pros and cons of each. Which option is more likely to best address your desire to be in this relationship and also address your concerns about career advancement and lingering resentments?

Agreement--In this case, the agreement refers to the solution you select after weighing the pros and cons. You are now at the place of discussing how you will implement the plan.

This is a version of the problem solving process used by mediators and peacekeepers the world over. It can be very helpful to use when you feel stuck. If after trying the process on your own you still feel stuck, you may want to seek outside help. All states have community mediation services. They are staffed by trained volunteer mediators and the mediation services are available to the public for minimal charges. Go to http://www.nafcm.org/public/findhelp to locate a community mediation center in your area. Remember, mediators are neutral. Their goal is to help you identify solutions to your concerns. Most of the time, mediators are able to help clients reach an agreement. And, in those cases when an agreement is not reached, most people find they leave a mediation session with a better understanding of the conflict and a new set of conflict management tools. I sincerely hope you and Arthur are able to find the best possible solution to your dilemma. It bodes well that you are both committed to the relationship.

Best wishes,

Dr. Amor

Reader Activities

Go to http://academic.engr.arizona.edu/vjohnson/Conflict ManagementQuestionnaire/ConflictManagement Questionnaire.asp and take the conflict styles questionnaire. Invite your partner to also.

Schedule a time to compare and discuss the results of the questionnaire. Create a warm ambience. Take turns sharing your results. Feel free to ask your partner questions about his/her results. Notice the strengths associated with that style.

Brainstorm and list ways you as a couple can become even more effective conflict managers.

Narrow the list to the top two ways.

List and discuss ways those two approaches will contribute to a healthy, happier relationship.

CHAPTER 4

Gratitude: The Power of Seeing Thought the Lens of Appreciation

Tip: Plant and nurture seeds of gratitude to strengthen and invigorate your romantic relationship.

Dr. Robert Holden is quoted as saying "The miracle of gratitude is that it shifts your perception to such an extent that it changes the world you see." Gratitude is one of many positive emotions. Simply stated, positive emotions are "feel good" states like joy, happiness, awe, serenity, and hope. Learning to cultivate "feel good" states is a step in the direction of living a more joy- filled life. Wouldn't you like to live a more joy- filled life? Wouldn't you like to energize and supersize your romantic relationship? Or, if you are single, perhaps you would like to strengthen your "gratitude muscle" as you prepare to re-enter the world of dating? I invite you to keep reading.

Awareness Matters

Several years ago, I sat on the doctoral committee of a student who conducted a study that examined things that influenced non-traditional student success in Allied Healthcare professions. Most of the students were women returning to school, after being out for a while, and many had already established families. The researcher hypothesized that social supports helped students succeed. What she discovered was -- it is not just how much support the students received that influenced their success. Rather, it was the *perception* of support that had the biggest impact on their success. In other words, perceptions trumped reality. Some students actually received little support, but their awareness of the support they received, and perhaps their gratitude for it, helped them accomplish their educational goals.

Students who, from an objective viewpoint, received much more support, but who did not perceive the help as support, did not benefit as much. This tells me that recognition and appreciation is key. Unrecognized and unacknowledged gifts and benefits do little to move us toward success and happiness in our endeavors.

The students in the study who did not recognize the help they received were not necessarily ungrateful. Instead, I think of them as having so much noise in the foreground of their thinking that gratitude as a 'thinking and feeling state' was drowned out. That is unfortunate on several counts. When we are not aware of the gifts we are presented with in life, we can be left feeling alone, unsupported, and deprived of the warm fuzzy, comfortable feelings that often accompany consciously receiving gifts. This is the question: How often do we overlook and disregard the bounty placed before us? And, what price do we pay for doing so?

Remembering

Let's think about this in terms of you and your partner. I have seen more than a few couples that come in with a laundry list of complaints about their partners. Common complaints are poor listening, controlling, too little sex, divided allegiances, and often enough - infidelity. Couples often have to be reminded of what they like or once liked about their partners. Perhaps we humans are wired to be more in touch with problems. Maybe being problem focused contributed to the species' ability to avoid danger. You know -- a survival technique. However, being overly focused on problems with one's partner does not work well in relationships. When we are overly focused on problems we, like the students in the study mentioned earlier, are likely to overlook many of the wonderful things the partner brings to the relationship. Simply stated, it helps to remember and be in touch with the good stuff. It is a matter of seeing the big picture.

Soon after beginning my work with couples, I encourage them to make a list of things they like and appreciate about their partner. Doing this helps them remember what they love or loved about their partner and helps us begin the couple's work, assisted by warm and fuzzy feelings that may have been drowned out by noise of the problems. I am often amazed by how helpful the conscious act of remembering can be.

Mindfulness

The thing is this-we have more choice over what we think about than we tend to take credit for. Think of it this way: We can choose to think about how he forgets to put the toilet seat down or we can choose to think about how he always gets the morning coffee going.

If we focus on the toilet seat, we are likely to feel annoyed. Focusing on the morning coffee is likely to evoke a warm feeling that might include gratitude. This does not mean that we overlook real problems or suppress feelings about significant matters -not at all. It simply means we are mindful of the numerous small gestures that can make us happy{ier} when we choose to be aware of them. Remembering gestures of kindness and being mindful of everyday expressions of love is likely to awaken feelings of gratitude. And, research has shown that positive feelings like gratitude have the capacity to build and strengthen social bonds and promote feelings of love and connection. Are you starting to see the role that gratitude can play in strengthening and invigorating your romantic relationship? The following note from Asia highlights the benefits of practicing gratitude.

Dear Dr. Amor,

I am writing to say thank you. Jon and I came to see you at a very low point in our relationship. So low, in fact, we were on the brink of breaking up. The sessions with you helped tremendously. I think the biggest take- away was learning to see the positives in this relationship, acknowledging them, and communicating them to each other. I have continued to keep a gratitude journal. Jon and I are engaged and plan to marry this fall. Who knew? I have a lot to be grateful for.

Asia

When Asia and Jon came for counseling they were experiencing some fairly serious problems. Despite the problems, they were committed to the relationship and were willing to put in the work required to resolve them. I was pleased to learn that months later they were doing well and continuing to use the tools acquired in counseling. During the counseling they experienced a shift in attitude when they were able to recognize the many ways they were happy with each other.

Jon and Asia experienced a shift in attitude and perception. Gratitude can, however, be thought of in many ways. You can think of it as a way of counting your blessing, an emotion, an attitude, awareness, or as a character trait or habit. I have come to think of gratitude as an awareness (of favor) that is a product of mindfulness. Gratitude as an awareness can transform into habit that gets hardwired into our way of experiencing the world. Who would not want to be more in touch with the ways we are nurtured and supported by the events and people in our life? Those of you who are currently in a relationship can choose to be grateful for the presence of your partner. You can choose to refuse to focus exclusively on those things about your partner that annoy and irritate you. You can commit to being mindful of both big and micro expressions of love and caring. I invite you to try it and see how it works for you.

Cultivating Gratitude

You may be wondering, "What about those of us not currently in a relationship?" The answer is simple. Now is the time, an excellent time in fact, to strengthen your gratitude muscle in preparation for your next relationship. All of us-currently in a romantic relationship or not, can stand to be reminded of the importance of gratitude and to learn ways of cultivating it.

Fortunately, more and more research is becoming available that helps us understand how gratitude relates to romantic relationships. Some of the findings are surprising. One researcher, Dr. Sara Algo (2010), found that when she asked her research subjects to imagine their romantic partner disappearing, they became more grateful for their partner. Clearly, the idea of loss stimulated appreciation and gratitude for his/her presence. She also found that savoring positive experiences with the partner encouraged feelings of gratitude. This can be done in daydreaming, journaling, or discussing a shared memory. Keeping a gratitude journal has long been considered a way of boosting gratitude.

Dr. Algo found that it is important to give your partner what he or she wants. I interpret that to mean when you compliment or praise your partner, do it in ways that matter to him/her. This relates to Gary Chapman's work as it is discussed in his book *The Five Love Languages:*

How to Express Heartfelt Commitment to Your Mate (1995). Chapman identifies five ways that individuals express and receive love, including spending quality time, speaking words of affirmation, offering gifts, offering acts of service, or physical touch.

It can help to know your partner's primary love language when it comes to expressing gratitude. Take, as an example, my partner expresses love through touch and enjoys being touched. Combining touch with a verbal expression of gratitude is the best way for me to communicate my appreciation of him. In comparison, I am deeply moved by words of affirmation. That means he is most likely to get my attention and deliver a full dose of gratitude by verbally expressing his gratitude to me in the form of affirmation - "You are so thoughtful. I really appreciate it when you ..."

So, to use gratitude to enhance your relationship consider adopting practices that grow gratitude:

- Recognize the importance of gratitude in enhancing and invigorating your relationship
- Be mindful of your partner's expression of love and appreciate it
- Recall and savor loving memories
- Consider keeping a gratitude journal
- Express appreciation to your partner in his/her love language

Reader Activities

Go to https://www.authentichappiness.sas.upenn.edu/testcenter and take the gratitude questionnaire.

Reflect on your responses.

Answer the following questions:

1. How will planting and nurturing seeds of gratitude strengthen and invigorate your romantic relationship? List three ways:

    A.

    B.

    C.

2. Think of a time in the last month when your partner did or said something that made you feel loved and appreciated. (If, need be extend the time beyond one month). The idea is to capture and reflect on the positive memory. Briefly describe the experience. Share this memory with your partner and invite him/her to share with you.

3. Think about the ways you like to be acknowledged and appreciated. Are you most sensitive to touch, affirmation, acts of service, or gifts? What about your partner? What is his/her preferred way of being

acknowledged? You may find it helpful to schedule a time to talk with your partner about this. Once you are aware of your partner's love language, make a point of using it when you express gratitude.

4. Identify one thing you are willing to take on that will help you stay mindful of the things you appreciate about your partner.

5. Share your thoughts about gratitude with one person other than your partner.

If you are working on gratitude but are not currently in a relationship, you can modify the questions. For example,

Question 1: How will planting and nurturing seeds of gratitude strengthen and invigorate your next romantic relationship?

Question 2: Think of a time when a partner did or said something that made you feel loved and appreciated.

Question 3: Think about the ways you like to be acknowledged and appreciated. Are you most sensitive to touch, affirmation, acts of service, or gifts?

Question 4, Identify one thing you are willing to take on that will encourage mindfulness and appreciation of the many positives in your life.

Question 5, Share your thoughts about gratitude with one other person. Ask that person for their full attention, and set aside a time and place where you will be uninterrupted.

CHAPTER 5

Forgiveness: Letting Go and Having More

"Your journey has molded you for your greater good, and it was exactly what it needed to be. Don't think you've lost time. There is no short-cutting to life. It took each and every situation you have encountered to bring you to the now. And now is right on time." ~~Asha Tyson

Tip: Practice releasing and letting go of old and new grievances, to allow your relationship to flourish. The key word is _practice_.

Opening to forgiveness is a process that promotes freedom from past grievances. Sometimes it seems to happen without much effort. At other times it is elusive.

Romantic Relations and Forgiveness

Have you ever thought of how forgiveness plays a role creating satisfying romantic relationships? Romance thrives in an environment where people are able to forgive and work through aggravations before they turn into huge grievances. When we do not have the tools, skills, and abilities necessary for working through grievances big and small, we are at a disadvantage when it comes to addressing the real and perceived slights that naturally come with being in a relationship. How many times have we heard it said that forgiving is for the benefit and well-being of the one doing the forgiving? There is truth here but only a partial truth. Why? Because forgiveness is beneficial for everyone involved - the aggrieved and the transgressor. I have seen countless people become motivated to forgive others after they have been reminded of what it felt like to be forgiven. Clearly, we all mess up from time to time and we all want to be forgiven. Getting in touch with the feelings that come with being forgiven can be helpful in your process of forgiving others.

The flipside of being forgiven is forgiving. The benefits of forgiveness are numerous. Benefits include freedom from resentments that can keep us stuck in the past, openness to the here- and- now with less focus on the past, and the possibility of creating new, exciting, and mutually satisfying romantic relationships.

Romantic relationships provide ideal breeding ground for hurt feelings, unmet needs, and disappointments. No surprises here. We all have conscious and unconscious needs that we expect our partner to know and meet, and many of us have particular sensitivities to intimacy that extend back to when we were children. What I am saying is this: occasionally feeling let down and disappointed by our partner is par for the course. As I discussed earlier, relationships are bound to hit rough patches from time to time. Knowing this prepares us to respond affirmatively when rough patches appear rather than becoming overly self-critical or overly critical of our partner. Awareness is good medicine that helps us avoid falling into dysfunctional ways of being. One dysfunctional way of being is holding on to grudges and resentments. So, while many of us think forgiveness is a good idea in theory, but becoming forgiving can be challenging even when you decide to forgive. Willingness is not always enough to rescue you from the snarls of unforgiveness.

In this chapter, we will explore the question of how to move away from smoldering anger, resentment, and bitterness directed at a present or past partner, and how to move toward being more forgiving.

Forgiving as a Process

Dr. Everett Worthington, (www.EvWorthington-forgiveness.com) a psychologist who has researched forgiveness for decades, has developed a five-step process called REACH. REACH offers a step process that helps people forgive transgressions:

R is for Recall. Recall the events and the hurt as accurately and objectively as you can.

E is for Empathize. Try to understand what happened from the point of view of the person who wronged you.

A is for the Altruistic Gift of Forgiveness. Recall a time that you hurt someone else and were forgiven. And offer this gift to the person who wronged you.

C is for Committing Yourself to Forgive Publicly. Write a letter of forgiveness (whether you send it or not), write in a journal, tell a trusted friend, or, if you can, tell the person who wronged you.

H is for Holding onto forgiveness. Forgiving is not forgetting. Memories of the wrong and feelings will come up. Remind yourself that you have made a choice to forgive.

Forgiving is a process. It is not, I repeat, not just mouthing the words—"I forgive you." How many of us remember as a child being told by adults in our lives to say "I am sorry?" It did not seem to matter whether we were sorry or not. Perhaps you were instructed to forgive and forget. How easy is that when feeling betrayed, deceived, let down and, and transgressed? In matters of forgiving many of us have much unlearning to do. To change from unforgiving to forgiving requires, in most cases, an awareness of the need and desire to forgive followed by laser- focused efforts to do so. Dr. Worthington's steps constitute a process that supports forgiveness. The process begins with recall of the events that caused you pain and ends with an ongoing commitment to choose forgiveness as many times as it takes.

Similarly, Dr. Robert Enright (2001) views forgiving as a process. His process promotes the idea of discovering the meaning of the suffering experienced as a result of the injury you want to forgive.

Dr. Robert Enright suggests a four-phase process in his book *Forgiveness is a Choice*:

- Uncover your anger; honestly examine the unjust act and your feelings about it.
- Decide to forgive; be willing to turn your back on the past and look toward the future.
- Work on forgiveness; forgiving is a process that takes recommitment and concrete actions.
- Discovery and release; be open to discovering the meaning of suffering, the need for forgiveness, the fact that you are not alone, and a new purpose in life.

Dr. Sonja Lyubormirsky (2008) offers additional exercises in her book *The How of Happiness*:

- Appreciate being forgiven; reflect on a time when you were forgiven; or seek forgiveness for a wrong you have done.
- Imagine forgiveness; imagine what you might say to the person and how you would feel.
- Write a letter of forgiveness; not necessarily to send, but to write out what happened and how it affected

you, what you wish the person had done, and end with a statement of understanding and forgiveness.
- Write the other person's apology letter; imagine the explanation the person would give for her behavior and how she feels about the harm she has done.

Remember, deciding to forgive is not the same as emotional forgiveness. Forgiveness involves a shift in how you feel and think. The story of Candace illustrates this point.

Case in Point

Candace, a 52 year-old widow, came to counseling seeking relief from the rage she felt toward her late husband. He had been a philanderer who had numerous affairs over the course of their marriage. He died unexpectedly six months before Candace came for counseling. She was surprised by the intensity of her feelings about her late husband. She found herself thinking a lot about the affairs, the lies, and the deception that came with his affairs. Candace struggled with these feeling for months before she decided that she needed help to work them through. Candace knew that her feelings were causing her emotional pain and she was concerned that her feelings of resentment and anger would interfere with her ever having a chance of falling in love again.

In time, we came to understand that Candace had never really forgiven her husband for his wrongdoings. She thought she had. Rather, she had packed away her feelings and learned to ignore them. She had unwittingly assumed the role of a long suffering victim. Our work in counseling involved unpacking the past, identifying and labeling her feelings, and discussing what authentic forgiveness would be in her case. After several months-- Candace reported that her nightmarish dreams of her late husband ceased. The stress of being in a chronic state of anger diminished and she was able to live more in the present. She decided that she would write a letter to her late husband explaining how she felt then and now. In the letter she discussed the ways his affairs had hurt her. She owned her part in her own victimization. Candace went on to set the intention of being open to being in a romantic relationship when the time was right. The last time I heard from Candace, she was engaged to be married. She was relieved that she had been able to do the work necessary to release and let go of the past in order to be fully present in the present.

Candace made excellent use of the counseling. She maintaining her here- and -now focus, even as she developed an awareness of how the past was influencing her present. Candace also avoided the potential distraction of focusing on her husband's behavior and getting bogged down there. The seemingly natural tendency to focus on one's mate, if left unchecked, can interfere with progress and lead to the erroneous conclusion that change is not possible.

Forgiving requires change and change can be tricky. Long established behaviors, attitudes, and perceptions may require greater effort to change than more recently acquired habits. Let's face it, those of us over fifty have had more than a little time to develop habits that don't always serve us well.

Despite the fact that some old habits aren't always in our best interest, change can be challenging.

Dr. James Prochaska's (1994) theory of change comes in handy here to help you determine how ready you are to change as it relates to forgiving. Prochaska identifies seven stages of change. Following are five stages that are key to forgiveness:

Stage 1: Pre-contemplation (Not Ready)

People at this stage of change are not prepared to make a change in the near future. Sometimes they are aware of the need for change, and sometimes not. Those who are aware may underestimate the pros of change and overestimate the value of staying the same. Pre-contemplators typically underestimate the value of change while overestimating the risks associated with changing.

If for any reason, you find yourself at the pre-contemplation stage of change, there are things you can do to move you in the direction of change. First, get clear about where you are stuck. Re-evaluate the pros and cons of forgiving. Envision your life free of the emotions that accompany unforgiveness. Consider revisiting the idea of forgiving within the next four to six weeks. Sometimes we have to plant the seeds of change a while before we see results of the effort.

Stage 2: Contemplation (Change on the Horizon)

In the contemplative stage, people are actively thinking about changing and are aware of the benefits in doing so. You learn about what you want to change. During this phase you may want to revisit the values involved in forgiveness. Is holding a grudge in keeping with my values or in opposition to my values?

At this stage of change, people are intending to start the new behavior within the next several months. They are, however, still considering the pros and cons of change and this can cause ambivalence. Left unchecked the ambivalence can cause people to put off indefinitely making the desired change. To avoid getting stuck in ambivalence, people can seek the assistance of others to help stay focused on the desired results of the change they are considering, and commit to taking small steps in the direction of the desired change.

In terms of forgiveness, people can make progress by starting with letting go of small grievances. Think of it as building forgiveness muscle. You start with light weight grievances and buildup to more substantial ones. Think about it. It does not take the same effort to forgive the neighbor upstairs for having a loud party than it does to forgive an ex-lover for dumping you without an explanation. Start where you are doing what you can do to develop an attitude of forgiveness.

Stage 3 Preparation (Getting Ready)

People in this stage are preparing for the change they want to see in their lives. They may be setting specific goals they want to achieve. It involves taking specific steps. People often begin to feel more competent in this stage. They may find themselves turning from a focus on the past to focusing on the present and the future. They may find themselves sharing their intentions with others.

Stage 4 Action- Time to Move

People at this stage have changed their behavior within the last 6 months and need to work hard to keep moving ahead. It is important for these people to do whatever it takes to strengthen their resolve to avoid slipping back into old ways of thinking and doing.

In my experience people in this stage can do several things to support their progress. They might, for example, keep a journal chronicling their progress. Another very helpful strategy is developing a loving kindness practice. Loving kindness meditation and affirmations involve affirming peace, happiness, and well-being for another. People at this stage should seek out like-minded people and avoid sharing their new behavior with people who are likely to be critical or otherwise unsupportive.

Stage 5: Maintenance - Staying There

People at this stage changed their behavior more than 6 months ago. They have maintained the changed behavior but it is important for them to remember that temptation abounds. They are still at risk of slipping back into old ways. They can support their progress by doing the things recommended in stage 4. Engaging with positive people in positive activities is highly recommended.

The following exercises are designed to help you move forward in your thinking about forgiveness and support you in your efforts to achieve the forgiveness you seek.

~

Reader Activities

For those of you who have forgiveness work to do involving romantic partners, I invite you to take the time to respond to the following inquiries

Based on Prochaska's stages of change where do you see yourself in terms of your readiness to forgive? What stage best describes you?

- Pre-contemplative
- Contemplative
- Preparation
- Action
- Maintenance

List three words that come to mind when you think of forgiveness.

- _____
- _____
- _____

What do those words say to you about your view of forgiveness? Will your thoughts about forgiveness support you or hold you back from forgiving?

Recall a time when you have been forgiven. What was it like emotionally, physically, spiritually, etc.?

- _____
- _____
- _____

Reflect on that memory of being forgiven. What do you notice about your state of mind when you think about having been forgiven? How does it feel?

Think of a person(s) or situation(s) involving a romantic breech where forgiveness has not yet happened:

(Select one person or situation to work with)

- _____
- _____
- _____

Personal Brainstorm (Jot down reasons it is important to let it go.) Really think about how you will benefit from releasing and letting go.

- _____
- _____
- _____

Recall a time you have forgiven another. What did it feel like emotionally, physically, spiritually?

- _____
- _____
- _____

Next steps: Based on your response, what now? For example, do you need more time to reflect on the benefits of forgiveness? Are you ready to decide to forgive? How will you support your effort to let go of resentments? Some people decide to work with a counselor or life coach to get the support they need to proceed through the process of forgiveness. Ideally, that person will have experience with romantic relationships and action planning.

Next steps:

- _____
- _____
- _____

Yes, you can put the past in proper perspective and create a new possibility for your present or future relationship by consciously choosing to let go of grievances that serve only to keep you locked in a story that no longer serves you.

Last but not least, remember to "Forgive yourself for not having the foresight to know what now seems so obvious in hindsight." -- Judy Belmon

CHAPTER 6

Staying Focused: The Power of Practice

Tip: Practice, Practice, Practice

Great, you are still reading! Because you are still reading, I am going to assume you would like to take your current or future romantic relationship to the next level of happiness. I have no doubt. You can do this! Remember, it is never too late to choose to do things differently. You bring a wealth of life experience and an awareness of your personal strengths that can be used to help you along.

Let's review. We have discussed ways of listening to your internal chatter that will benefit your efforts to get the love you want. As I discussed earlier, the gremlin, sometimes referred to as the internal critic, can wreak havoc on romantic relationships. The gremlin is skilled at sending subtle and not so subtle disempowering messages. Counter intuitively, listening rather than attempting to ignore the gremlin is the best approach. Listen with the intention to reassure the gremlin that you are capable of adequately addressing its concerns. Show it that you understand gremlin speak. For example, when the gremlin whispers "all your relationships have ended badly, give up on relationships and take up knitting" by shifting your perspective you can come to understand the gremlin as a part of yourself concerned first and foremost with your well being. Rather than viewing the gremlin as an unwelcomed saboteur, you can choose to see it as an alarm system sounding the alert when it perceives you to be at risk emotionally. By reminding the gremlin of your capacity to learn from past mistakes and apply new learning, you can soothe its concerns, and in so doing, quiet its mumbling.

We also discussed the importance of sound communication. Imagine the difference it would make in your relationship if you were to speak your truth with openness, honesty, bravery, and compassion? Taking it a step further, imagine if you DECIDED, that no matter what, you would honor your commitment to communication with truth, honesty, bravery, and compassion.

When it comes to conflict, most of us have a preferred way of responding. Sometimes our preferred way of responding is the best way under the circumstance - other times not so much. Learning your conflict style can go a long way toward helping you become aware of your habitual way of responding to conflict while offering you new and different strategies for managing differences. Since conflict is inevitable in interpersonal relationships, our best bet is to learn to manage it effectively. So, I provided several tips in chapter three on how to manage conflict effectively. Equally important is perspective. If you have not done so already, I invite you to think of conflict as an opportunity. How is that, you might ask? When you and your partner manage conflict well you are left knowing that the relationship is strong enough to weather a disagreement without tearing it asunder. Remember, this can be very reassuring to a couple still assessing the viability of a relationship, or reassuring to an established couple testing new waters.

In chapter four, we discussed ways that gratitude can enhance and deepen romantic love. Gratitude is such a powerful emotion. The following quote by Dr. Robert Holden shows just how impactful gratitude can be: "The miracle of gratitude is that it shifts your perception to such an extent that it changes the world you see." Now, *that* is a powerful statement! This is a quick activity to test his observation. Close your eyes. Without much thought think of something you are unabashedly grateful for. It can be a person, place, thing, or state of being - whatever. Make an effort to envision it in your mind. Focus harder and really give it detail, sound, feeling, scent, etc. Once you have fully formed the memory or image savor it. Momentarily, just be with the experience. Now, notice your feelings. Chances are you experienced a positive emotion. Maybe you felt:

- Happy
- Joyful
- Grateful
- Generous

and/or, a host of other positive emotions. Practiced on a regular basis, you will see how being in touch with things we are grateful for creates an internal shift in the direction toward positive feelings.

Chapter five explores the value of forgiving. The discussion examines the value of forgiveness, barriers to forgiveness, readiness to forgive, and strategies for supporting your effort to become a more forgiving person.

There you have it! Five tips that, if utilized on a regular basis, will significantly enhance your current or future romantic relationship. I promise, if you practice these strategies on a regular basis you are bound to see a positive difference in your romantic relationship and in your life as a whole. Ginny and Joan's story illustrates this perfectly.

When Ginny and Joan came for premarital coaching they were feeling discouraged and disheartened about their relationship. They had been in an on again, off again relationship for years. They had two children, and more than anything they wanted to make the relationship work for the sake of their children. They identified sexual incompatibility and extended family issues as major concerns. Our initial discussion revealed that the problems were long- standing and deep- rooted. Despite their pessimistic view of the relationship they were committed to show up and work hard in hopes of salvaging the relationship.

True to their word, they showed up for every session with homework completed. They demonstrated a willingness to be open, honest, and vulnerable. We worked on communication, conflict management, and gratitude. Several months later we agreed that they were in a good place and had the tools and skills necessary for meeting whatever challenges would come their way in a lifetime of togetherness. The following year I received a note from them:

Dear Dr. Amor,

Thank you for helping us with our relationship. What a difference a year makes. Our children are thriving and our relationship, is solid. We enjoy each other's company and continue to apply the strategies we learned in our coaching sessions. Our biggest take away is the realization that each of us needs to concentrate on our own healing. We are no longer the blaming, responsibility- avoiding people you met over a year ago. With your help we created a vision of how we wanted our relationship to be . We are living that vision.

Testimonies like this remind me of why I am passionate about this work. As Ginny and Joan become skilled in being in relationship their children are positively impacted. Each generation thereafter benefits from the success of the previous generation, and so it goes.

I sincerely hope you have found some of the ideas and practices discussed here helpful. I am on a mission to share with all of you what I have learned in over thirty years of clinical practice, hoping we can add to the joy, peace, and love available to us all. Be brave, lean in, and go for it, making the world a better place, one relationship at a time.

About The Author

Pauline G. Everette, LMSW, PhD is a relationship coach and counselor. She has been in private practice for over 30 years helping individuals and couples create the lives they desire. She specializes in coaching couples who seek to repair and/or revitalize their romantic relationships. Dr. Everette and her husband of over 40 years live and work in Detroit, Michigan.

Keynote

Finding and Keeping Romantic Love: Relationship Tips for People Over 50 offers strategies for energizing your current relationship and/or preparing for your next romance.

Utilizing key exercises that help you personalize and apply the tips you will come to realize that romantic love and romance are possible even when you have given up hope of finding that special someone.

Six easy to follow tips are presented along with an action plan that will help you get busy creating the romance of your dreams.

www.ingramcontent.com/pod-product-compliance
Lightning Source LLC
Chambersburg PA
CBHW030523290526
45786CB00004B/1598